Body Systems

The Respiratory System

Why Do I Feel Out Of Breath?

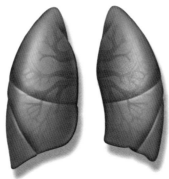

Sue Barraclough

Heinemann Library
Chicago, Illinois

© Heinemann Library 2008
a division of Pearson Inc.
Chicago, Illinois

Customer Service 888-454-2279

Photo research by Hannah Taylor and Maria Joannou
Designed by Debbie Oatley and Steve Mead
Printed and bound in China by South China Printing Company

ISBN 978-1-4329-0870-6

12 11 10 09 08
10 9 8 7 6 5 4 3 2 1

Library of Congress Cataloging-in-Publication Data

Barraclough, Sue.
    The respiratory system : why do I feel out of breath? / Sue Barraclough.
        p. cm. – (Body systems)
    Includes bibliographical references and index.
    ISBN 978-1-4329-0870-6 (hc) – ISBN 978-1-4329-0876-8 (pb) 1. Respiration–Juvenile literature. 2. Respiratory organs–Juvenile literature. I. Title.
    QP121.B25 2008
    612.2–dc22
                                2008001158

Acknowledgements
The publishers would like to thank the following for permission to reproduce photographs: ©Alamy Images pp.**22** (David R. Frazier Photolibrary, Inc), **24** (Elvele Images), **27** (John Fryer); ©Corbis pp.**4** (Dimitri Iundt), **26** (Dimitri Iundt, TempSport), **14** (Heide Benser, Zefa), **10** (Image Source), **12** (Luca Tettoni); ©Getty Images p.**6** (PhotoDisc); ©Punchstock p.**7** (Blend Images); ©Science Photo Library pp.**9** (Damien Lovegrove), **16** (Martin Dohrn, Royal College of Surgeons), **19** (Susumu Nishinaga)

Cover photograph reproduced with permission of ©Punchstock (Blend Images).

Every effort has been made to contact copyright holders of any material reproduced in this book. Any omissions will be rectified in subsequent printings if notice is given to the publishers.

Disclaimer
All Internet addresses (URLs) given in this book were valid at the time of going to press. However, due to the dynamic nature of the Internet, some addresses may have changed or ceased to exist since publication. While the author and the publishers regret any inconvenience this may cause readers, no responsibility for any such changes can be accepted by either the author or the publishers.

Contents

Some words are shown in bold, **like this**. You can find out what they mean by looking in the glossary.

What Is My Respiratory System?

You breathe air in and out of your body through your nose and mouth.

Your respiratory system is the parts of your body that help you breathe. There are parts you can see such as your nose and mouth.

There are also parts inside your body that you cannot see, such as your **lungs**. These and other parts make up the respiratory system.

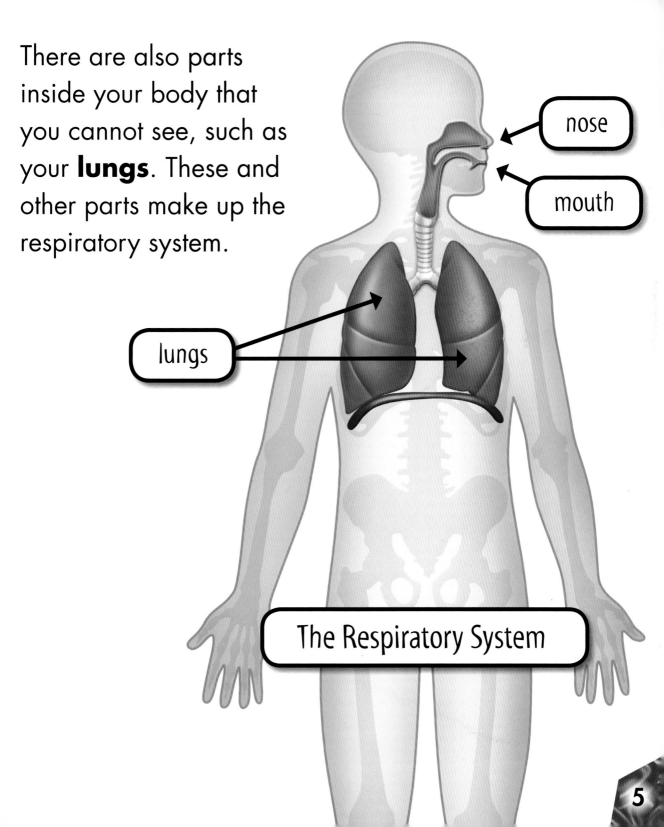

nose

mouth

lungs

The Respiratory System

Why Do I Breathe?

Oxygen and **carbon dioxide** are gases in the air that you breathe. You breathe because your body needs to take in oxygen and get rid of carbon dioxide. You breathe air in and out without needing to think about it.

You breathe ⇨ air in and out all the time, even when you are sleeping.

You can control your breathing. You can breathe out
air to blow up a balloon. You can hold your breath
for a short time under water.

How Do I Breathe?

You breathe by pulling air into your nose or mouth. **Muscles** in your chest move to pull air in. The muscles push air out again as you breathe out.

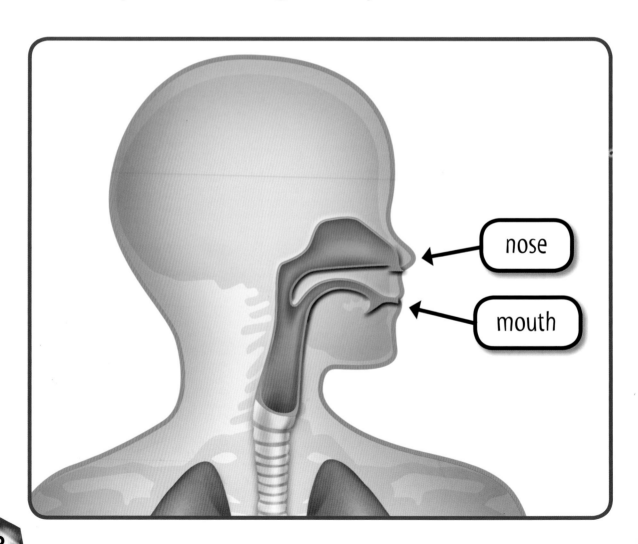

nose

mouth

⬆ **Sometimes you sneeze if too much dust and dirt goes up your nose.**

Sometimes you breathe in dust and dirt. Tiny hairs in your nose catch dust and dirt. The hairs stop dust and dirt from going into your body.

What Is My Windpipe?

Your windpipe is a tube that connects your nose and mouth to your **lungs**. The air travels from your nose and mouth into your throat. The air then passes through your windpipe into some smaller tubes and then into your lungs.

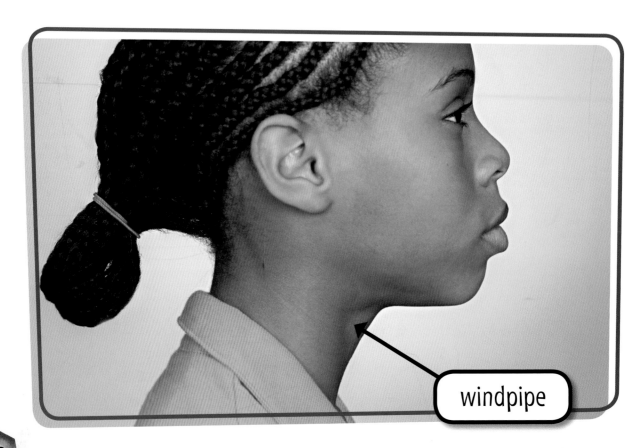

windpipe

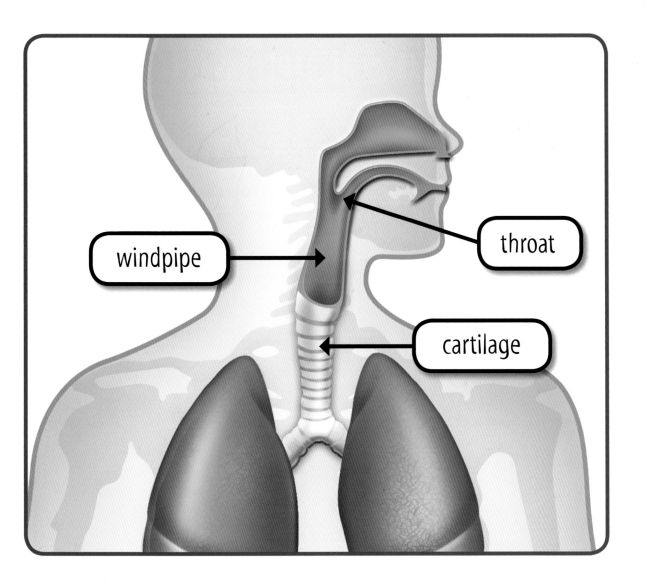

windpipe

throat

cartilage

The windpipe is lined with **cartilage**. Cartilage is strong, stretchy **tissue**. It is found in joints and other parts of the body such as the nose and ears. Cartilage keeps the windpipe open all the time.

What Is My Diaphragm?

Your diaphragm is one of the **muscles** you use to breathe. Your diaphragm is under your **lungs**. When you breathe in, muscles on your ribs pull your ribs out and up. At the same time your diaphragm moves down, and this sucks air into your lungs.

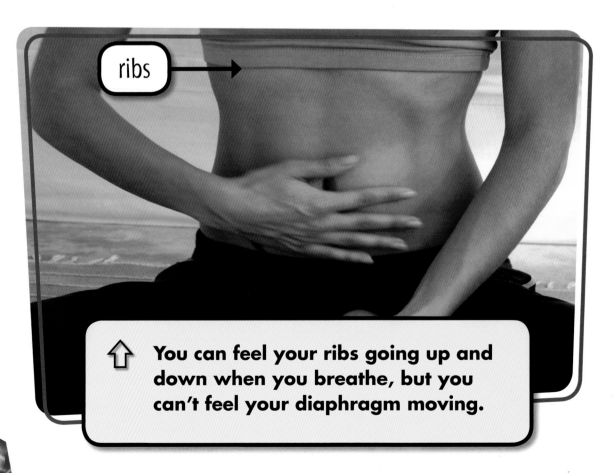

ribs

⬆ **You can feel your ribs going up and down when you breathe, but you can't feel your diaphragm moving.**

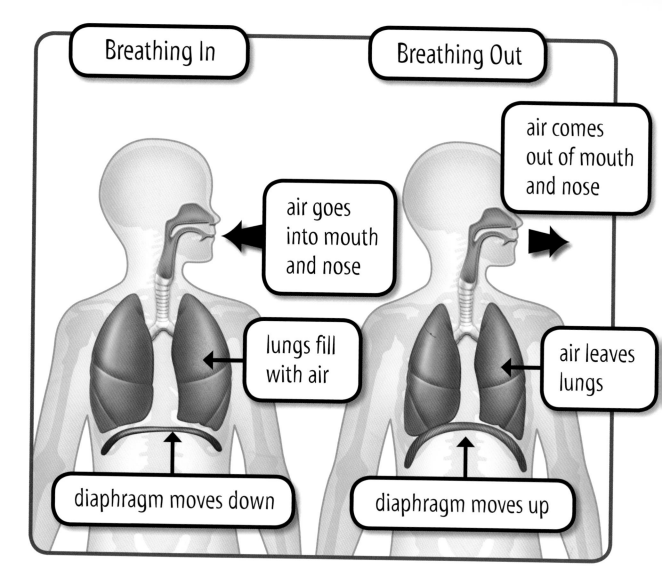

When you breathe out your diaphragm pushes up. Your rib muscles push your ribs together. This changes the shape of your chest and squeezes air out of your lungs.

What Are My Lungs?

Your **lungs** are two spongy **organs** that fill most of your chest. An organ is a part of your body that is made to do a certain job. The job of your lungs is to take **oxygen** from the air you have breathed in and to get rid of **carbon dioxide**.

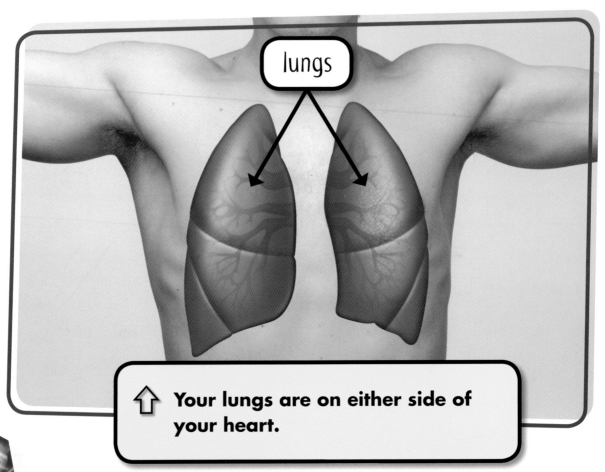

lungs

⬆ **Your lungs are on either side of your heart.**

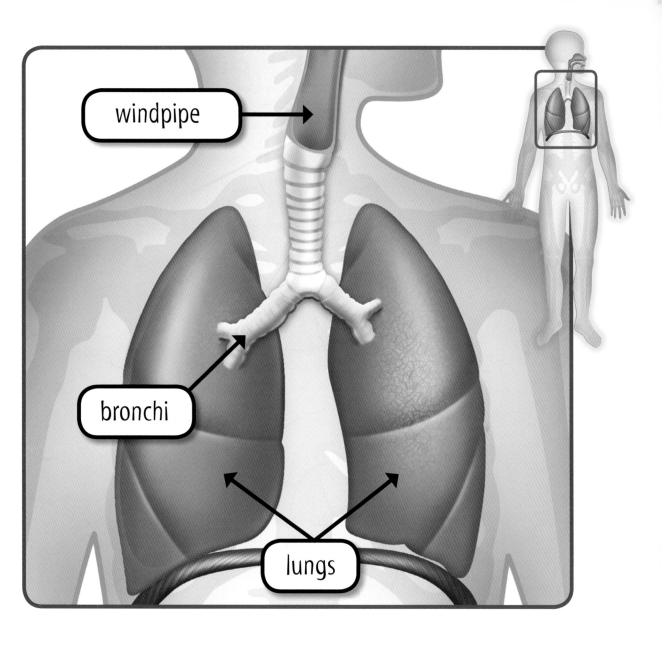

The air goes down the windpipe. The windpipe splits into two tubes called **bronchi**. The bronchi carry the air into the lungs.

How Do My Lungs Work?

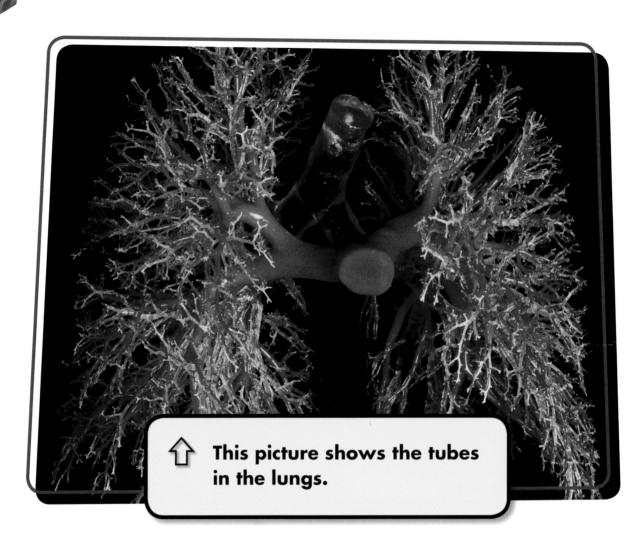

⬆ **This picture shows the tubes in the lungs.**

The **bronchi** tubes split up into smaller and smaller tubes. The tubes fill your **lungs** like the branches of a tree. These tubes are called the bronchial tree.

The smallest tubes of the branches have a bunch of **alveoli** at the end. Alveoli are tiny round bags that fill with air. **Carbon dioxide** moves out of your blood and into the alveoli. The alveoli take the **oxygen** from the air that you have breathed in.

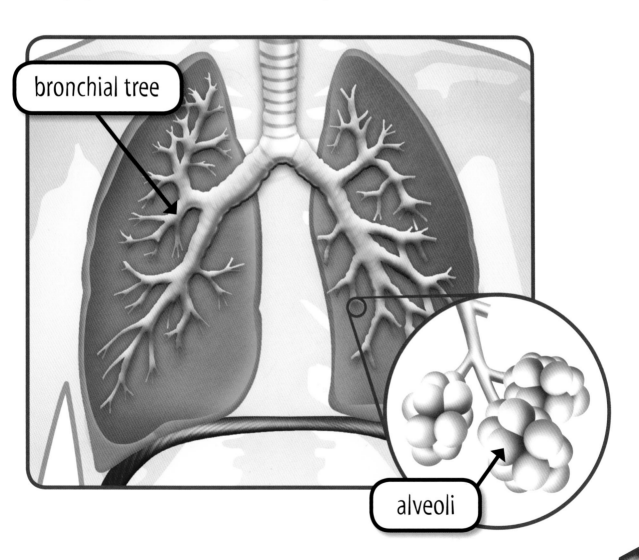

bronchial tree

alveoli

How Does Oxygen Get into My Blood?

The **alveoli** are covered in tiny **blood vessels** called **capillaries**. Blood vessels are tubes that carry blood. Capillaries connect your **lungs** with the other blood vessels that carry blood around your body.

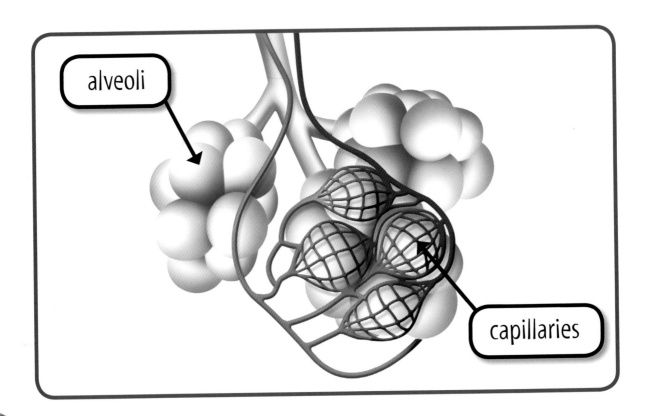

alveoli

capillaries

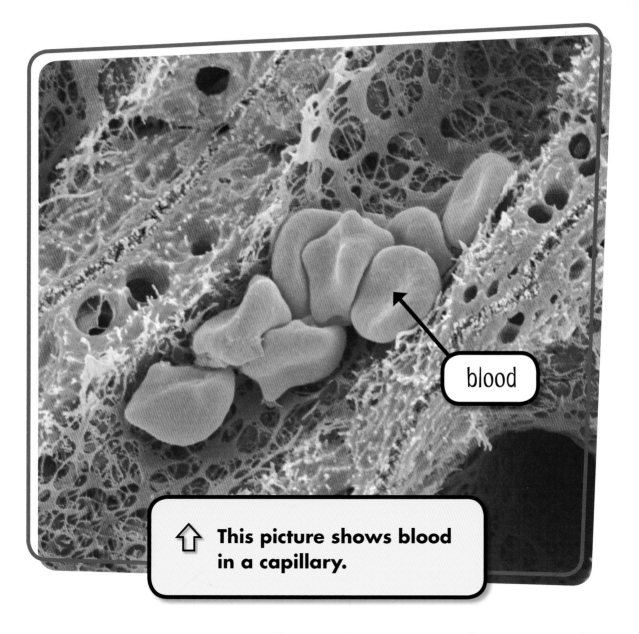

blood

⬆ **This picture shows blood in a capillary.**

Oxygen goes through the thin walls of the alveoli. It goes into the blood in the capillaries. The oxygen is carried to your heart in your blood.

How Is Oxygen Used?

Blood full of **oxygen** is pumped out of the heart. The blood travels round your body in **blood vessels**. Oxygen passes from your blood into your **cells**. Cells are the tiny living parts that fit together to make your body. Cells use the oxygen to get **energy** from your food.

Producing energy makes another **gas** called **carbon dioxide**. Carbon dioxide is a gas that your body cannot use. Carbon dioxide can be harmful to your body.

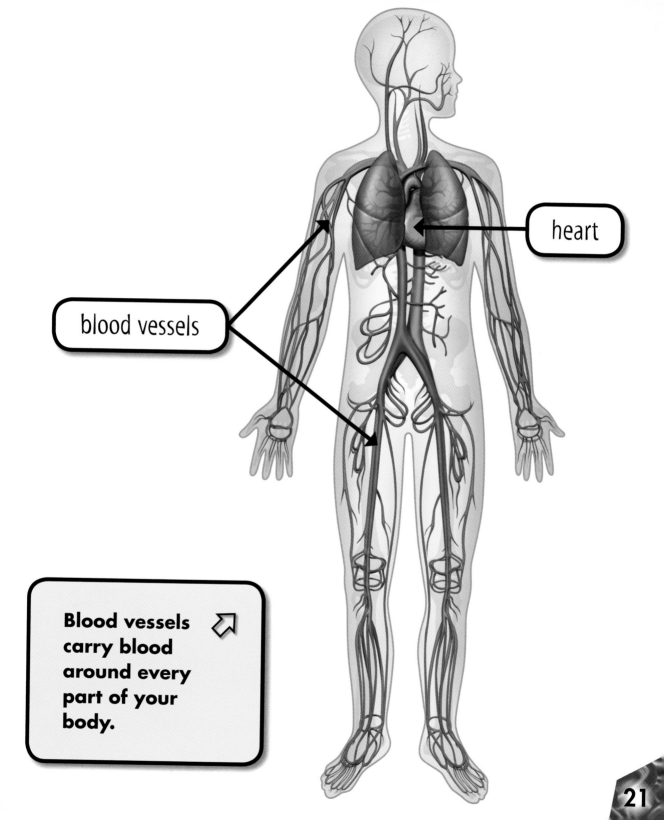

heart

blood vessels

Blood vessels carry blood around every part of your body.

Why Do I Breathe Carbon Dioxide Out?

Carbon dioxide is bad for your body so it must be breathed out. It passes out of the **cells** and into the **blood vessels**. Blood carrying carbon dioxide travels back through your blood vessels.

Breathing out pushes carbon dioxide out of your body.

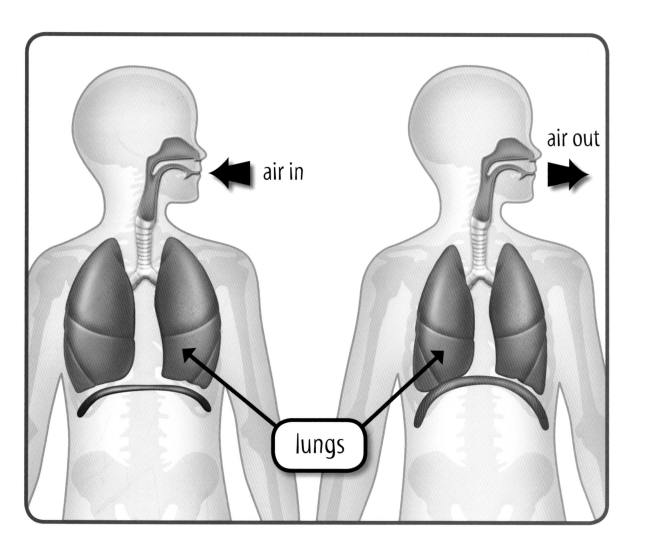

air in

air out

lungs

The carbon dioxide is taken back to your **lungs**. The lungs move air carrying carbon dioxide out of your body when you breathe out. After carbon dioxide is breathed out, air carrying more **oxygen** is breathed in.

The Respiratory System

Your respiratory system works non-stop to keep your body working. Your brain, **muscles**, and all your body **cells** need **oxygen** to get **energy** from your food so they can work properly.

All the parts of your respiratory system work with your heart and blood system to take oxygen to every part of your body.

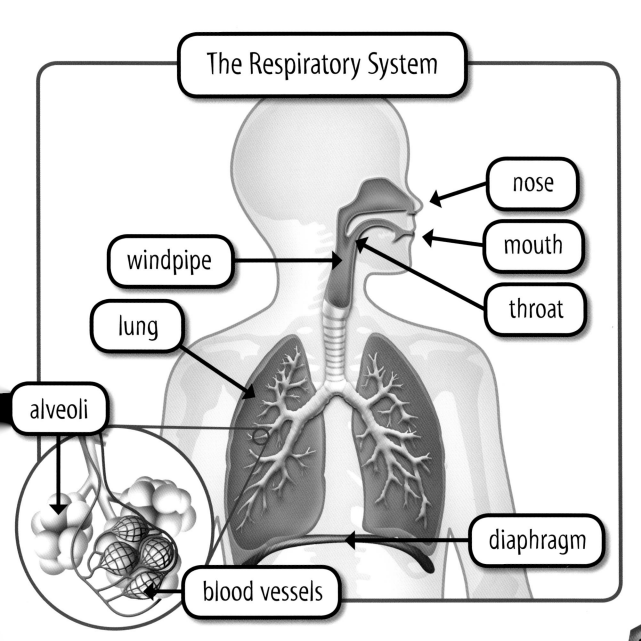

The Respiratory System

nose

mouth

throat

windpipe

lung

alveoli

diaphragm

blood vessels

Why Do I Feel Out of Breath?

When you exercise you need to breathe in **oxygen** faster. This is because your **muscles** and other body parts need more oxygen to produce **energy**. Your body needs to get rid of **carbon dioxide** quickly, too. So you need to breathe in and out faster.

⇧ **These runners need to breathe fast to keep their bodies moving.**

↑ **These runners made their hearts and lungs work very hard.**

Sometimes you cannot breathe in and out fast enough. So you feel out of breath. This may be because your heart and **lungs** are not strong enough. If you exercise more, your heart and lungs will get stronger. This means they can work faster and you will not get so out of breath.

Did You Know?

The **lung** on the left side of your body is a bit smaller than the lung on the right side. This makes room for your heart.

You breathe in and out around 20 times every minute.

A part of your brain called the brain stem controls your breathing.

Plants take in and use the **carbon dioxide** we breathe out. Plants then make **oxygen** that they release into the air for us to breathe in.

At the back of your mouth there are two tubes. The esophagus is for food and the windpipe is for air. When you eat, a flap called the epiglottis covers the windpipe so that food doesn't go down into the lungs.

In your throat is a part called the voicebox. This helps you talk. As you breathe, air passes over parts called vocal cords. This makes sounds. You can control how the air moves over the vocal cords to talk.

You get hiccups when your diaphragm jerks suddenly, sucking air into your lungs. It may happen when you drink a bubbly drink, laugh a lot, or eat too quickly. Nobody really knows why it happens.

Glossary

alveoli   parts of your lungs. They are tiny round bags that fill with air.

blood vessel   tube that carries blood

bronchi   tubes that carry air into your lungs

capillary   tiny tube that carries blood around your body

carbon dioxide   gas that your body needs to get rid of

cartilage   type of strong, stretchy tissue. It can be found in joints and other places such as your nose, throat, and ears

cells   tiny living parts that fit together to make your body

energy   power used to make things happen. Energy can make things grow, change, or move.

lung   organ in the chest used for breathing air in and out

muscle   stretchy part of your body that tightens and relaxes to make movement

organ   part of your body that has a certain job to do

oxygen   gas found in the air that your body needs to stay alive

tissue   group of linked cells in your body

Find out more

Books to Read

Harker, Leslie and Pat Thomas. *My Amazing Body: A First Look at Health and Fitness*. London, UK: Hodder Wayland, 2002.

Royston, Angela. *My Amazing Body: Breathing*. Chicago: Heinemann Library, 2005.

Seymore, Simon. *Lungs: Your Respiratory System*. New York: Collins, 2007.

Websites

http://www.kidshealth.org/kid/htbw/lungs.html
Learn about your lungs, what your respiratory system is and how it works. Find out what you can do to help keep your lungs and respiratory system healthy.

http://hes.ucf.k12.pa.us/gclaypo/repiratorysys.html
Find out how the respiratory system helps you to breathe. Look at fun facts about the respiratory system. Find out the answers to questions such as "Why do I yawn?," "What causes hiccups?," and "Why do I sneeze?".

http://science.nationalgeographic.com/science/health-and-human-body/human-body/lungs-article.html
Choose "lung functions" and move the diaphragm down to see how the lungs and the respiratory system work.

Index